PARENTING YOUR ATHLETE

***

Dr. C.E. Andrews

PARENTING YOUR ATHLETE

ISBN-13:9780692458761

ACKNOWLEGEMENT

There are so many to acknowledge, but most of all I want to say thank you to my children, Brian, Phillip, Justin, Larissa, and Karlan. They taught me so much about life through their participation in sports. Thank you, thank you, and thank you. But I also have to say thanks to the coaches and others who took part in the development of this booklet:

Coach Bob Verissimo	Golden West High School CA
Coach Chuck Mosley	Woodlake High School, CA
Coach Steve Harrow	Golden West High School, CA
Coach Tom Donald	Buchanan High School, CA
Lucas Kephart	University of Texas
Kirk Ashe	Former Professional Baseball Player
Darin Moore	Former Professional Baseball Player
Tim Ryerson	President STUDENTathleteWorld
And to all the others who helped	

PARENTING YOUR ATHLETE

A LETTER TO THE PARENTS:

Greetings parents,

This little booklet was written with you in mind. It's not intended to tell you how to parent or how to raise your child. Its sole purpose is to assist you in evaluating and encouraging your student athlete to their greatest heights.

It's not about one particular sport, but sports as a whole. All sports are as equally important to the development of our youth. Not all children develop a love or desire for a sport, but I believe it's important to have them participate for their own growth and development. Your child may not be the next "Home Run King" or "Super Bowl" winner or even a "Gold Medalist," but so much can be gained through their participation in sports.

No matter what sport, and there are many to choose from, it's the same advice for all of them, ENCOURAGE, don't push, don't demand, and don't pressure. Your student athlete will do plenty of that on their own. You may be asking; *then what should I do?* Be their cheerleader, their number one fan. You know, the one who picks them up when they're down and slaps a high five on them when they're up? But most of all, be their parent.

Sit back and enjoy your children and don't be surprised if you learn a thing or two about life as they get involved in sports.

Dr. C.E. Andrews

Introduction

I believe every parent whose child participates in sports should read this booklet. I've done my best to make it fun and easy to read. While I touch on some tough issues, I trust the humor will put a smile on your face. Remember, this is not an exhaustive study of each topic we touch. If something I've written makes you stop and think, then I would encourage you to research it more in depth.

Just in case you haven't heard or seen, sports have become a huge part of our society. Youth sports programs have grown so large that it takes up a great part of our children's lives for most of their preteen years. While programs have grown, so have the issues and it's time to address a number of them. Therefore, one of many reasons for this booklet.

Before I go any further let me tell you a little about myself. I love sports, all sports, well almost all sports, now days there are some things called sports that are borderline as far as I'm concerned, but I won't get into that. I have so many wonderful memories from my childhood and most of them center around sports. You know what I mean, playing catch with my dad, tossing the football around, and roller skating as a family. Those will never go away and I wanted that for my children. That's one reason I encouraged them to participate in organized sports from a young age. I desired them to have those memories about us, like I did with my dad.

As a parent I was blessed as they made all-star teams, played on travel teams, played through high school and college. We had great family times together. Those are etched in our minds forever; no one can take those memories away. I learned so much from these many adventures, not only about myself, and other parents, but the impact sports can have on these young adults, both good and bad. That's another reason I need to write it down.

I've coached at different levels leading up to college. I've sat on Boards, raised funds, been involved with boosters and most anything else you can think of. I've traveled across this beautiful country with teams and parents. Yes I've been a parent in the stands, (and at times not a very good one, *sorry coach*), a coach in the dugout, had disagreements with parents, officials and anyone who would listen, lol. So, yes I have been where you are right now and I wouldn't trade it for anything.

The last reason I wrote this booklet is that I want you as a parent to enjoy your time with your children. I am older now and spend a lot of time reflecting on those days we had together and I know they do too.

So, sit back, grab a cup of coffee or a Starbucks and enjoy, but most of all, learn from others mistakes and don't do what we've done.

Enjoy

SECTIONS

"Do you know what my favorite part of the game is?
The opportunity to play."
- Mike Singletary

WHY SHOULD THEY TRY SPORTS?

The opportunity to play, wow, do we really look at it that way? With sports being such a large part of the American culture, we sometimes forget that it is just a game and taken far too seriously. Why? My educated guess is, because of all the money being thrown around. That's a totally different topic and I don't want to get side tracked, so, back to why kids should play.

When the topic of playing sports comes up, we think of the popular ones; football, baseball, basketball and soccer. If we stop there though, we miss so many other opportunities. For example there are some that are offered in our schools; swimming, track, cross country, etc., while others are found in the general public; karate, roller skating, ice skating, and gymnastics, just to name a few. There really is something for everyone, and it's really just a matter of your child's needs and/or desires.

Playing a sport should be fun for both the parent and child. It's a great way for your child to build confidence and also provides plenty of opportunity to teach them about discipline and life.

Many believe, me included, that sports play an important part in young people's physical and mental development. Here is what Marianne Engle, Ph.d., a sports psychologist and Clinical Assistant Professor at the NYU Child Study Center, has to say:

"About 20 million American children ages 6 through 16 play organized out-of-school sports, and about 25 million youth play competitive school sports; 30 to 45 million kids ages 6 through 18 participate in at least one school or community-based athletic program."

So, with so many children playing sports growing up, if her stats are correct and I believe they are very close, we need to take a closer look at the overall goal of these activities. Most of us want our children to be their own person, to stand tall, be self-reliant and to find success. While playing sports won't guarantee these things, it will give them a great head start. It's a solid base to provide those to our kids and help with their healthy development through life. The problem I've observed is that a lot of the time parents get in the way of their child developing these traits.

So to assist you, I've gathered a short list of attributes and defined each one to make sure we are all on the same page. The list is as follows: Confidence, Social Abilities, Responsibility,

Leadership, Teamwork, Competition, Diligence, and Sportsmanship. So here we go:

Confidence: the quality or state of being certain.

That's what's so great about participating in sports; it gives quality of assurance of a job accomplished. No matter if one wins or loses. You may be asking yourself, *"How can you say that losing builds confidence?"* If you did, then you must have forgotten or didn't read the quote from Mike Singletary, "Do you know what my favorite part of the game is? The opportunity to play." We parents seem to lose this far too early in our child's sport life. Make this your goal, to remember how blessed your children are to have the opportunity to play sports. If you instill that, and the fact they can finish a task, their confidence in life will begin to flourish. There is nothing more exciting than to see the face of a youngster hitting the ball for the first time or making that goal.

Social abilities: being able to blend into society.

Sports allow children to learn social skills. They learn how to interrelate with other children and watch other families interact. They learn how to deal with success and failure. The wonderful thing about sports is they cross all social lines, race, economic and language barriers.

Responsibility: a duty or task that you are required or expected to do.

Sports, if we as parents allow them to, teach our children responsibility, what it means to make a commitment and to stick with it no matter what. They may not like their coach or another player, but when they stay with it, they learn. As they do this, we as parents also learn new valuable lessons.

As your child grows older, the role of a student-athlete becomes increasingly important. The ability to balance out sports and school will instill responsibility in the child, allowing them to plan accordingly. We all know the importance of education in our children's lives and we're still learning the importance of sports to a child's physical development. Becoming a student-athlete gives emphasis to the importance of combining academics and sports. In fact, education at the high school and college levels require the combination of the two to compete. Thus making a child ineligible if their grades are not up to the standards of the school. With proper balance of the two, by being responsible in their choices, makes success is much easier to achieve.

Leadership: a position as a leader of a group.

Your child will also learn the characteristics of leadership through sports and the importance of it. Not everyone is made to be a leader, but sports teach each child about leadership. Whether to be a leader, or how to pick which ones to follow. A leader will quickly evaluate his teammates and will come alongside of each. With talent being wide spread it's the fun part about learning to be a leader. It teaches how to make adjustments for each individual.

Teamwork: the combining of individual efforts to accomplish a task at hand.

This one is number one for me, the main teaching point of sports is, teaching your child how to work with people; from coaches, to parents, to teammates, working together towards the same goal. It's a social skill that so many lose out on. It teaches how to depend on someone else and how to allow other people to depend on you. You can see it early on in soccer for example, the kids all go after the ball, not knowing about teamwork, but as they grow and learn they start to trust their teammates. A skill they will cherish for the rest of their lives as they move out into the job market.

Competition: the act or process of trying to get or win something (such as a prize or a higher level of success) that

someone else is also trying to get or win: the act or process of competing.

Life is about competition. We do it in our daily lives, whether it's for that job you want, or the promotion. It's all about competing. If we fail to teach our children and young adults about competition, when they go out into the world, they will have a difficult time adjusting. One team wins and one team doesn't, one person gets the promotion or job, while the other one doesn't. Those are difficult lessons to teach, but vital for your child's growth. We must assist them to learn from those defeats, how they help us get stronger and push forward to that next level of our lives. Competition should make us ask, *'What more do I need to do to gain the advantage over my competitor?'*

Diligence: careful and persistent work or effort.

This is an area we all probably need a little encouragement in, to be diligent in all we're doing. No matter if it's taking out the trash or running a marathon. Diligence is something we need to be doing and teaching our children. While that's all good and easy to say, the difficult part is to continue to be diligent when we are up against a wall or obstacle in our lives. It's pretty simple to move forward when things seem to fall into place, but for most of us, when something unexpected pops up we begin to take a few steps back. However, a fine-tuned athlete has been trained to push forward no matter what. An example of this is a distance runner who pushes through a portion of his race when he has, as the expression goes, "hit the wall." Diligence at its finest. Our youth need a large dose of diligence, well, in fact, our society really does.

Sportsmanship: fair play, respect for opponents, and polite behavior by someone who is competing in a sport or competition.

Here is another all important topic to train our children in. It's not winning at all costs. It's sportsmanship at all costs, even if it means losing the game. The older I get the more I dislike professional sports and the main reason being, the lack of sportsmanship. With all the trash talking going on and showing up the opponent, it's getting out of hand. And our youth are seeing this and practicing it in their sport. We as parents need to curb this behavior.

I watched a video that you may have seen too, it showed the opposite of what I mentioned. It happened during a college softball game. A young lady hit a home run to put her team ahead. When she rounded first base she hurt her knee and fell down. It was so bad she couldn't walk. According to the rules, if her teammates were to help her, the run wouldn't count. So as she laid there hurting two opposing players picked her up and carried her around the bases, stopping at each base making sure she touched it. Now that's sportsmanship. The parents of those two girls did a great job teaching them about the value of sports.

Okay, now that we have touched on a few of the character issues sports help to develop, let's take a quick look at how sports helps our children to mature physically and mentally.

Physically: We have become a lazy society. We all know how important physical exercise is for any age and most parents want their children to be fit. However, according to a 2013 survey done by AC Nielsen Company, the average youth spends 900 hours a year in school and 1200 hours a year watching TV. We as parents are failing in this area. What's the answer? Get them involved in sports. If you train them to be physically active in the early stages of their lives it will prove to be beneficial as they grow.

There are three competitors out there robbing your child of an active life, TV, video games and cell phones. Now, there is nothing wrong with any of these, until that's the only thing your child is doing a majority of their time. We know through surveys that during the childhood years, normally between the ages of 6 and 11, the child's body goes through multiple changes. If you encourage and keep your child active during this time it helps achieve a healthy pattern for life in him or her.

Mentally: The mental aspects of all sports can be as beneficial, if not more, than anything else. Building confidence and self-esteem in your child is a trait that will take them through life with their heads held high.

Keep in mind that your child must also understand the middle ground of winning. It's not everything, and it shouldn't be. Winning is nice and can build confidence, but knowing to get right back up and shake it off if you lose is another strong characteristic to have. Winning should coincide with the other elements of sports such as teamwork, fun, fitness and confidence. Make sure your child understands that it isn't about winning; it is about how you win. Some people will do whatever it takes to win, including cheating, and that is a negative developmental characteristic. When your child enters sports, make sure they embrace and celebrate winning, but don't overemphasize it as the most important aspect. Winning with class and dignity is the most rewarding victory.

When your child plays sports, they will develop a high multitude of positive characteristics that will carry them throughout life; not just in the field, court, or ring, but in everyday living.

Exposure is important, and not just in the sports you're interested in. Your child will naturally gravitate to your likes and dislikes. If you want proof, just look around. You don't often see a young child and parent rooting for different teams. They are usually on the same page. Now that may change as the child realizes that they can choose for themselves, but generally speaking they stay with the one team.

***

LIFE STORY: My two older boys, love playing sports and still do even into their late thirty's and early forty's. I always encouraged them to try new things. Besides baseball, my major sport was roller hockey, since I lived in California and there wasn't ice skating within a reasonable distance I gravitated to roller hockey. So as the two boys grew they played soccer and both were quite good (starters on their high school team) and my oldest even playing at the JC level. Once they were able to choose for themselves they also began to play roller hockey, and still do. I encouraged them to try them all, just like I did with all my children. I am proud to say that I believe that sports taught them the work ethic they now have. They understand that to get anywhere in life they have to work hard at what they are doing. The work ethic behind being successful in sports bleeds over into our everyday lives. What is success? Is it playing in the pros? It could be for some. The World English Dictionary states it this way, "the favorable outcome of something attempted." A favorable outcome for youth playing in sports is being able to participate. It's finishing the race, finishing the season no matter what the record is. Here's one thought to finish this section on, in competition, someone always comes in first and someone places second, but the real story is finishing no matter what. A few years back I watched the Ironman triathlon. The time to finish the race had come and gone and there were very few people left at the finish line. One gentleman never gave up and crossed the finish line without the accolades of a crowd or a television crew to interview them. Why didn't he just quit and walk off the course? Because he wanted to finish no matter what. That's what we should be teaching our youth. FINISH NO MATTER WHAT!!!!

STARTING OUT:

You picked this booklet for a reason. It may be you're a parent, grandparent or relative with a young athlete, or teen playing a sport. It may be that your child may be too young to play, but you're looking ahead at the possibilities. There are so many ways to start, but just remember as you start, set out a few goals. Not what you want to accomplish but what it is you want to help your child accomplish. If you read the introduction it will help you set forth those goals. So many times I have seen parents have goals for themselves instead of for their child. You know what I mean, let's get a college scholarship, or play varsity ball in high school. With a younger child just starting, the focus should be fun and evaluation. Evaluation you ask? Yes evaluating, not just their talents in the sport, but how much fun they have playing. As their parent, you should encourage them to try all different sports, even sports outside the norm of school. I loved playing baseball, but also enjoyed roller skating and playing roller hockey. My mother, a single mom, did all she could to encourage me in all that I did. So as you and your child start out in the wonderful endeavor of sports, remain open minded, never berate one sport over another. Find something they enjoy and the only way of doing that is to assist them to search them all.

So how do you start? Well, by knowing your child. What are their interests; not only in sports but what do they like to do? If it's just sitting around the house, then get them going in some activity. Watch some sports on TV with them, take them roller skating, to the park, kick a ball around, and just be active with them. If they like to tumble, help them. All I'm saying is that you need to be an active parent. We all have the same excuses, work, not enough time, too busy, or whatever we want to use, but remember that your child will never be the age they are again. I realize not every parent can be so involved, but just do all you can to be there for them. You will look back on those times and it will bring a smile to your face and be a point of conversation as they grow into that man or woman that you can be proud of.

***

LIFE STORY: I was coaching a 13 year old travel baseball team and lost a few players. So, I did what most coaches do and advertised a try-out. I had numerous players come to the try-out and I talked with each family after. One young man wanted to make the team so badly that he brought a resume for me to look over. He was a year younger than the other boys and not as talented but his enthusiasm made up for it. I explained, to him and the family, that by being younger and not quite at the talent level of the other boys he wasn't going to get a lot of playing time. His dad, (a very wise man and encourager to his son), said, "We know he won't play much, but I want him around young men like these so he can see how hard they've worked to get here." Well, what could I say? The young man played well when he got the opportunity and the other boys enjoyed having him around so much so that they would go to his Little League games. That is what parenting is all about. Putting your child in a relaxed position to learn all they can. I am so thankful for the example this couple gave to the other twelve families on the team.

ENCOURAGE YOUR ATHLETE

Boy, I don't think I can say this enough, encourage, encourage, encourage. Young people and especially young athletes put enough pressure on themselves to succeed that they don't need parents adding to it. They want to make you proud of them and when they, so call, fail (in their eyes), they experience a minor form of depression. In order to understand how to encourage I want to explain ways we discourage our young athletes. So many parents make the mistake of discouraging and they're not even aware of it. My recommendations are simple; don't make statements or comments, ask questions. Be a good listener, the old saying is, *"God gave you two ears and one mouth for a reason, listen twice as much as you talk."* Then, don't tell them how you think they did; ask them how they think they did. Depending on your child, they will focus on the failures, most humans do. Remember, they will always be harder on themselves than you. By doing this you teach them how to evaluate their performance and gives you a great opportunity to help them do it properly, which will be important as they grow. Pick out things that they tell you, especially the negative things, and encourage them through it by pointing out the good things they did. This helps them out of this habit. While learning from our mistakes is very important, a total focus on them is just as damaging. Again, ask good questions; what could you have done differently? What would you change if you had it to do over again? Encouragement comes in all forms, so be that parent that comes along side of your athlete and helps them deal with the disappointments of life. All the while, teaching them how to deal with them.

One coach put it this way: *"Always be their #1 fan. If they fail, they need encouragement, not a play-by-play breakdown of their failure. Don't compare them to other sibling's (or parent's) accomplishments if applicable."*

A second said, *"One thing parents can do to support/encourage their athlete is by not pushing them into something they don't really want to do...another way of showing support or encouragement is to seek help from a specialist coach (hitting/pitching coach/lessons or whatever sport offers side lessons)...a third way of encouraging their athlete is offer to send them to a sport specific camp (baseball, football , volleyball, etc..) a final way of showing support/encouragement is to just be there for them...don't be their coach...they already have one...parents need to be the safe haven for their athlete and not another coach to evaluate their performance after another contest."*

One college player put it this way, *"be encouraging and give them confidence, teach them to work HARD and get after it, and teach them to be disciplined and self-motivated."*

One of the aspects of encouragement is teaching our children how to deal with failure. As with our lives, failure is a big part of your children's life, and at times we have unrealistic expectations of our child's abilities, not only in sports but academically. Our expectations of our child bleed over to them and when they fail they have the feeling of disappointing you and when they tell us, our response will either encourage them or disappoint them.

We must understand then explain to them that as long as they prepared themselves to the best of their ability there really is no failure. As the college student athlete stated above, *"teach them to work HARD and get after it,"* then the results are what they are. So, if they don't get the grade on the test they wanted, ask them questions like; what can you do better next time? Did you really put in enough study time for the test? Can you honestly say you totally prepared for this?

So many times children aren't taught how to study. They go through the motions and they think that if they spend enough time with their books open that it will help. Sometimes it's laziness, but I believe most of the time they have never been taught how to study. The earlier they learn the more they will develop. It's just like sports, the more someone participates the better they will become. Now they may not develop into a star player, but they will improve.

***

LIFE STORY: Expectations, we all have them, no matter what age you are. We place them on ourselves and on others. Whether at work, home, school or in sports we are guilty. Come on admit it! That's 90% of anything, admitting when we do something or have done something wrong. So now that you've admitted it, what do we do about it? The first thing is to not put those expectations on your young athlete. They already do! How many have played in the back yard and pretended to hit that home run to win the World Series or score that winning touchdown in the Super Bowl? Most young athletes have those dreams. When we place expectations on others we set them up to fail.

This is done all the time in the corporate world too. Promoting people to a level of incompetency without the proper training or instructions or talent evaluation (this will be covered a little later). This is a vital part of parenting your child through sports. We, as parents, tend to believe our child can do things that they really aren't capable of doing. So instead of encouraging we place expectations on them. There can be a fine line between the two, encouraging them to compete the best they can or placing unrealistic expectations on them. Take an honest look at yourself, which are you doing?

I was told a story of a coach who was coaching in a championship game. They were on their way to winning the championship and there was a young person who, let's just say, wasn't as talented as some of the other children, but wanted to be part of the team so badly. The coach decided to put him in, to the displeasure, I will say, to many of the parents in the stands. As things go, the young player made a critical mistake at the wrong time and cost the team the championship. With the parents in the stands grumbling, (I can't imagine that happening), the coach took the kids to the middle of the field and told them that every player tried their best and it was only a game. He went on to name each player and tell them how proud he was of them. Then he said, something I think is awesome, but sad at the same time, "If your parents say things about losing the game, tell them, that all of you tried your hardest and that the coach is proud of all of you." It's a shame a coach has to be the parent at times, instead of just being the coach.

WHAT ABOUT BURNOUT?

I was never one to put much credence to this statement and that was to my shame. Yes, there is such a thing as "burn out". As I researched this area I found an abundance of ideas and advice. The best definition I could find comes from sports psychologist: "physical/emotional exhaustion sport devaluation and reduced athletic accomplishment.[i]

Athletic participation is both physically and emotionally draining, so as a parent you have to maintain close observation of your child. Author R.H. Cox in his book, *Sport Psychology: Concepts and Applications*, list three things to watch for; "Excessive stress and pressure, the feeling of entrapment and the issue of empowerment."

Let's quickly examine these three comments:

Excessive stress: With youth sports today there's a lot of unnecessary pressure to win. A lot of coaches have too big of an ego and winning becomes all about them. They don't understanding the huge responsibility they have in helping to form young men and woman into productive adults. With this pressure the young men/woman may become stressed which will eventually lead to physical and mental fatigue.

The feeling of entrapment: This usually comes from within the family. The parents and athlete have invested a lot of time, money and energy into the sport, therefore the athlete feels trapped. They don't want to let the parent down but they no longer experience the joy from playing and they begin to grumble and complain about anything involving the sport. Even winning doesn't change their attitude. They need a break or the ultimate cost may be the loss of desire to play any longer.

The issue of empowerment: Sociologist Jay Coakley proposed the idea that the structure of organized, competitive youth sports becomes controlling. It controls the identity of the participants and controls their lives, leaving them feeling disempowered. Coakley theorizes that a desire for personal control over one's life is a possible cause of burnout in youth sports.

Burnout has been found to be more active in children who have chosen to be a one sport athlete. This would mean they probably play their sport year round.

When we talk about burnout the ultimate danger is the young athlete dropping out of sports all together, so we want to identify the different signs and indicators of burnout. In their books, *"Athlete Burnout: Potential for research and intervention strategies"* and *"The Athlete Burnout Syndrome: A Practitioner's Guide,"* L. K. Fender[ii] and S. L. Cresswell, & R. C. Eklund[iii], identify two areas to be aware of when you think you may be dealing with burnout. To eliminate confusion I have included all the authors' thoughts together.

The physical realm is identified this way: *"tension, fatigue, irritability, decreased energy level, problems sleeping, increased occurrence of illness, inconsistent performance, and exhaustion."*

Next they looked at the Behavioral indicators of burnout: *depression, feeling helpless, anger, feelings of disappointment, and feeling that one's contribution to the team is insignificant.* Cresswell and Eklund also pointed out, *"... that some of the symptoms such as depression can occur independently of burnout."*

As a parent remember, that as your child begins to develop and grow, their interests may also change. Don't try and alter this change, allow this growth to happen.

As your young athlete enters middle school and high school they are exposed to different sports, allow them the opportunity to experiment if they so desire. You may even encourage them to expand their horizons. As a sophomore in high school I wanted to do something different so instead of playing baseball I ran track, even though I wasn't very good at it.

One coach put it this way, *"Give the kids a break! Not all sports need to be played year around. They don't HAVE to choose a sport by age 5. Let them be kids!!!!!"*

Another well respected coach said, *"(That's) easy, don't play year round...players get stale, the same muscle groups get overworked/abused...kids need variation...kids need different challenges physically and mentally from various sports or other sports related activities...I cringe when I hear of 9 year olds playing fall ball and not flag football or cross country.. LET THEM BE KIDS...we aren't doing fall ball next year...we are going to concentrate on weight lifting and speed development...I think our kids will be excited about the start of baseball season."*

***

LIFE STORY: *I wish I had remembered the old saying "variety is the spice of life." Yes I fell for the lie that your child has to be seen to get any offers. Now we had great times together and met a lot of wonderful people who are still friends, but at what cost. I tried to encourage my son to play other sports in high school, but by that time I had already done the damage. I kept telling him that he can't go back and do it over again and I didn't want him to regret not playing other sports.*

Today, year round sports is the norm. While years ago athletes were able to play multi-sports, it is much harder today

than ever, thus we get the term 'burn out.' We wonder why kids get burned out on a sport and people shake their heads and try to push the blame on everyone else, instead of looking at themselves. As far as I am concerned there is plenty of blame to go around. From parents having unrealistic expectations, to high schools doing their scheduling, to colleges and their dumb rules and regulations. Burnout is real, no matter how much the child loves the sport. So give them a break and have them try other sports and things. I know what you're saying, "but they have to earn that college scholarship." Let me share something with you, when it comes to college or pro sports it's all political. Don't fall for, "You have to get them out there to be seen." You can spend a lot of money "getting them seen," and it won't do much good. Now you can have some great times with your kids, but don't fall for the trap that they have to stay active in the sport for them to get offers. In fact, I think that the more sports they are able to participate in, shows a well-rounded student-athlete. So the best way to avoid burnout is to encourage and maybe push them towards other sports or music, or whatever.

GAINING PERSPECTIVES ON MY CHILD'S TALENTS

This is one of the most difficult topics to write on and one of the most difficult things for you as a parent to do. One coach even suggested, *"Nothing. Do not attempt to gain perspective. Instead just realize that as a parent it's impossible to have perspective and be ok with that. Cheer on your child as a fan and realize you are irrational and cannot judge between YOUR child and others."* Again, that is easier said than done. As your children progress through the school years it helps in the evaluation process. Once they reach middle school and high school, sports becomes more competitive. They have to deal with tryouts and possibly not making the team. Don't panic if this happens, if your child is really interested in the sport encourage them to work a little harder and come alongside and help them.

I can tell you who not to ask, lol, grandparents, uncles, aunts or any other relative. They are always bias as you will be toward your child, that's what makes this so difficult. Parents need to step back and enjoy their children participating in sports. At the younger years it doesn't really matter who is better. What matters is the development of your child.

Now, your child may be a really good athlete as he competes with other kids his age or he may be in a small community and one of the better players. To gain a proper perspective of their talents we must ask for other peoples input and then expand our evaluations by competing in a larger area. Most parents have blinders on when it comes to evaluating their child's athletic abilities. They think they are the best thing since sliced bread.

A coach, I have the utmost respect for, shares the following with the families who talk about playing at the next level, *"I've always told parents to go watch a college practice or a practice at a high profile high school to see what the talent level is and what it takes to get to the next level...talk to a scout and get an honest evaluation of their child's talent (don't ask the guy who is giving you lessons...he/she will tell you good things to keep you coming back for lessons...seen this happen A LOT) I went to Cary, North Carolina last summer and helped pick the Team USA 18 Under National Team...invited 144 players from around the country to try out for the team...first cut of players to top 40 was very difficult and then had to cut that down to the top 20 players...now there were some seriously talented kids/players who didn't make the team.. we sent home players with Div.1 scholarships...they could all play, legit D-1 guys...it would have been great for my parents to see just what it takes to be a Div.-1 guy."*

This coach is a great evaluator of talent and a great coach. Why do I say that? Not because his teams are always one of the best in his area, but because he gives the families direction on how to help their child be all they can be. Not every child is a Division 1 talent and he will tell them that up front in a gentle and kind way.

Another coach I highly respect suggested this, parents must *"Realize that a very small percent of players make it to the very top levels of any sport (D1, Pro, etc). Ask your kid's coach for an honest evaluation of the strengths, weaknesses, and where to work... Have an outside coach (not affiliated with your child's team) evaluate your child."*

Finally, we have to make the parents understand that as the student advances, and this is in any sport, the physical skills of the players become better and more equal. Eventually the student athlete will hit a level where their child can no longer compete at the same level. As their parent you must help your athlete to be mentally conditioned for this to happen.

I will close this section with a statement from a former professional ballplayer that also played in college. *"Although I am not a parent this has to be one of the hardest things they have to do for their children when it comes to sports and 'reality'. I think parents need to listen to coaches and also be real about how good their child is. If their child is not one of the top player's stat wise on a team, they probably won't have opportunities at the next level, i.e. high school player getting a chance or scholarship to play in college."*

***

LIFE STORY: *I want to share a time I took my son to a Showcase. Now, we were told to go to as many of these as possible to get the maximum exposure. So not knowing any better we set out to accomplish the task. One of our first ones was in Southern California and with about another 100 young men. If I may say this now, Showcases are okay to go to, but don't expect much from them. Now, I'm sure there are ones out there that are good, but be picky if you decide to go that way. I would recommend getting someone on your side to help you through the process. Wish I would have had someone. Anyway back to the story. We get there and spend the first morning going through the normal workouts, but there's a rumor going around about some young man coming in the afternoon. Later that day they divide the young men into teams as this young man arrives. The Showcase directors take time out so he can work out and take batting practice. Well, let me tell you this* *young man was impressive. He was heads above anyone else there. It was wonderful for myself and my son to see and be able to evaluate his talents against the other young men. Just an FYI this young man is presently playing in the major leagues.*

WHY NOT COACH? (YOUR INVOLVEMENT AS A PARENT)

I enjoy coaching and realize it's not for everyone. I love kids, their enthusiasm, energy, and for the most part their drive. While coaching isn't for everyone, how do you know it's not for you if you never try? I knew nothing about coaching soccer until my two youngest decided to play and they needed coaches. So I stepped up and coached both, my daughters and sons teams. It was a blast! I researched drills and talked to other coaches. I learned more than the kids did. I coached every year for the next five.

Like I said not every family can coach, but every family can be involved one way or another. Too many times sports are used as a glorified babysitter and the coach has these children for an hour or so and it doesn't cost the parents anything for a sitter. If you do that, shame on you! Now, if you're doing other things for the team or league then you're covered. Every youth organization needs help, get involved. You can sit on the Board, help organize some part, help with the team. All you have to do is ask and they will find something for you to do.

A high school coach put it this way, *"Parent involvement comes in the form of fund raising... which supports all the kids in our program by helping us with our fund raising efforts (dinner, snack bar, summer tourney, etc...) coaches coach, players play, parents cheer...don't be a helicopter parent always hovering around your child...they will never fully develop as a person if you (parents) are always around fixing everything for them...leadership skills will never develop if parents organize everything (play dates, play time, games in the neighborhood)...stay away and let them grow up."*

Oh, and another thing, if you complain about the refs, umpires, or whatever, then step up and do the next best thing, do it yourself. Most people who complain about the refs don't understand how difficult it is. Half the people aren't going to like you no matter what you call. Besides, most of the people who complain don't know the rules. Refs aren't perfect, and they are human, so make sure you treat them that way. When was the last time you told them thank you? Your child will miss a basket, strike out, fumble, or make a bad pass; in other words mess up. The coach will make the wrong move, (at least in your eyes), or call the wrong play, in other words mess up. So why do we think an umpire or ref should be perfect? Here's a shock statement, "THEY WILL MESS UP." So expect it, if you're a coach, teach it. To start the season I would ask my players a list of questions and one being, "What is the strike zone?" Each year after a number of players try to explain it to me I'd tell them this, "Whatever the umpires' calls." This is with all sports, it's unfortunate at times, but the way it is, even in the pros. So live with it.

Being involved with youth sports is one of the most rewarding things anyone can do. So step up and enjoy.

***

LIFE STORY: This is a short story about a child and their team without a coach. At the time, I was on the league board and assigned to help find coaches for the teams without one. So as any good volunteer does, I jumped on the phone and started making calls. Right around the, oh I don't know, between 15th and 20th call I finally got a dad to talk to. I explained the situation to him and he responded, "Oh I couldn't possibly coach, I don't know anything about the sport." I reassured him that we would help him all we could and that we also offer coaches clinics before the season started. He gave me a couple of more excuses, but as any slick salesperson does, I rebutted each one. Finally, and I will say reluctantly, he agreed. We met the next day; I once again thanked him, and then gave him an outline of how to run a practice and his equipment. With excitement in his voice, he told me he had searched the internet and found all sorts of instructions for running a practice. Now, I wish I could tell you that his team ran off with the championship, in fact that would make a great movie, but they struggled all year. I saw him at the end of the year and he was eager about coaching the next year.

You never know what can happen and how much you can grow by stepping out and being available. Now that's not the end of the story. A number of years later I ran into him in the mall and we stopped to talk.

One of the first things he said was "Thank you for pushing me into coaching. I have had so much fun."

"Are you still coaching?" I asked.

"Oh yes, having the time of my life." He responded, "In fact I've gotten more involved and I'm a Sectional Director now."

I'm sure my jaw dropped as I thought, here's a man who didn't know anything about the sport, but stepped out of his comfort zone to help the kids and now is having the time of his life. WOW!!! Who knows, the time of your life may be just around the corner, why not test the waters and get involved? It's just a phone call away.

WHAT NOT TO DO AS A PARENT?

This could be a really long chapter as I have seen and been told a lot of horror stories. This question in my survey got the most and longest answers. As I funneled through the answers there were a few that always seemed to come up; be the parent, encourage your student athlete and let them have fun.

We are going to take a look at a few of the top answers, so here it goes.

Don't live your life through your child. I have seen this over and over again. One college athlete put it this way, *"Knowing when to be involved and when to back off...it's a fine line and a tough one to walk."* No better words could be said. As a former athlete it is difficult to walk that line. We make excuses for our involvement: we want our child to have a better chance at it than we did. I'm just trying to be there for them. Or whatever you want to say. As parents we try to rationalize away our actions.

One of the most common issues is some parents get too involved and stunt a players/child's social growth or fight battles for their child when they should be the one to ask the coach about playing time.

The next issue that needs addressing is, don't play politics to get your child playing time. A prime example is a story I was told about with a high school coach being forced to resign because parents went to the Athletic Director and complained because of some made up reason. When in fact the reason was their children weren't getting the playing time they thought they should be.

That leads us right into the next thing not to do which we touched on already so won't go into a greater detail, unreal assessment of their child's talent. This is very common and you may need to re-read the section on this.

Next, don't be too hard on them, no matter what the age. Failure is a great learning tool and they aren't professionals. Assist them in learning from their failure and sometimes it's just the way things go. Nobody plans on failing. It's nothing we wake up in the morning thinking about, *"Oh, let me see how I can go out today and fail at the things I do?"* One of the best parts about sports is that it teaches how to be competitive and how do deal with failure. Those who are taught how to handle losing graciously will go so much further in life than those who don't.

Another short story I want to share is about a team, very talented travel team, who seldom lost. Their talent was exceptional all the way through the roster, in fact, most of the players on this team went on to play college ball. Anyway, they played a team from a smaller area and during the tournament crushed them. As fate would have it this small area team made it through the brackets and faced this other team again in the championship game. The small team turned the tide on them and ended up winning the championship. After the congratulations were all done, the coach on the other team said, *"Pack it up boys, we aren't staying for the awards, we only except first place trophies."* Now that coach may have later talked to his team, I wasn't told if he did or not, but he allowed a wonderful opportunity to slip through his fingers to explain the rewards of losing.

A former pro athlete put it this way, *"The biggest thing that I believe parents can do is teach their children how to deal with failure. I probably have a biased opinion to baseball but so much is centered around failure in that sport and how you respond to it."*

Please, don't make excuses for your child's failure. If they make an out, miss a basket, or drop a pass, maybe it just happened because the opponent was better. It isn't anybody's fault. Stop babying your child! If you make excuses for them your teaching them to make excuses, don't do it!

So that's a few things of what not to do. How about a few of what to do: Teach them to be "coach-able", also show up on time, and get rest. Most importantly, do not ignore academics.

Teach them that when they are in the public or at school, they represent their team so act accordingly—people are always watching and what you do affects your teammates, the coaches and the program.

Another survey got this answer. *"What did I try to do as a parent?" I learned with my first son that I was too hard on him at times and tried to stay off my second son but didn't always do so...I tried to be supportive and I let them fight their own battles...I didn't coddle my boys and tried to teach them to respect themselves, others and the game. I tried to teach them not to cut corners and to be worker Bee's. Ultimately I tried to teach them to keep everything in perspective and they are a son, brother, uncle, friend, Christian and not just a baseball or football player. Too many parents/kids think their identities are wrapped up in their success on the court, field, gym, etc. it's just ONE part of you, not the total package."*

***

LIFE STORY: I had an experience both growing up and one from a coaches perspective. The growing up one first, there was a child I knew who loved playing sports and was very talented, would have probably gone places if it wasn't for his dad. I will call him Martin, not even close to his real name.

Anyway Martin was an exceptional athlete loved basketball and baseball. His dad was one of those over bearing dads who pushed and pushed, you did notice I didn't say pushed and encouraged. There is a huge difference! Well, one day we are in a game and Martin does something wrong can't remember exactly what it was and it doesn't really matter. Well, his dad marches out on to the field and grabs his arm and takes him off the field straight to the car and leaves. I was so embarrassed for him. Martin now over the next couple of days would have to face all of his friends and teammates. At that point in time I remember thinking, I sure am glad I don't have a dad like him and was really thinking I was happy I didn't have a dad at home.

The next story comes from a coach's perspective: Let me start by saying this, you as a parent are entrusting your child to the coach. If you have an issue with what he is doing, please go to him when he is alone and not after or before a game. Hopefully, the coach has clearly expressed his rules to all the parents and has opened things up for discussion. I say that to say this, a coach needs to know that the parents are with him, he is not perfect and will make mistakes just like we all do, but he is taking his time to commit to teaching your child how to play the sport, so please respect that. There is an answer to a disagreement between you and him, coach yourself. Now back to the story, one evening the coach was wrapping up practice and had the players out on the field for some final drills. One parent took it upon herself to walk out on the field and tell two boys to go get in the car that practice was over for them. The coach politely told her they were about done to allow them to finish the drill. The parent told the coach that this was her son and he was leaving, along with the other child, because she was told to pick him up. The coach didn't argue with her, but it did affect the other players and again I felt sorry for the young boys, who would have to face their peers again at the next practice.

My last story is quite the opposite. A coach gave me this story and I thought I would share it. He was coaching a JV team and this player was one of his top players. The young man had one drawback, his dad. It seemed like when the coach would tell the young man to do something he would ignore him and look at his dad. The season was winding down and this young man was playing pretty well and was probably going to get called up to varsity for the playoffs. The last game the coaches had talked it over and there were a couple of young men that hadn't started a game all year and they had worked hard at practices. So the coaches decided to start these players and sub later in the game. Well this didn't go over very well with the dad or player. The coach explained the situation to the player, but it didn't matter he still pouted while on the bench. His dad came over and talked to him and still no change. Later he was inserted into the game and made three crucial mistakes that ended up costing them the game. After the post-game talk as the coach was leaving, the dad approached him about his son. The coach explained the situation and left. Later that night the coach got a text from the parent blasting his decision and stating his sons stats compared to the other boy. This man's son had started and played each inning in every other game. Needless to say the young man didn't get called up. It's not always about playing ability a lot of times it's about attitude and are you a team player. Are you willing to sacrifice yourself for the good of the team?

As I surveyed the different coaches they placed parents into three categories. It's kind of like Clint Eastwood's movie, *"The Good, the Bad and the Ugly."* I have summarized these three areas, read them and probably reread and see where you fit. You may be a combination of two, a little of this and a little of that. If so, it's okay, just make some adjustments and all will be good. So read on and find out where you are now.

THE GOOD: Not much to say to this one. This is a parent who has a proper perspective of sports. They may understand the game and may have possibly coached at some point. They want to help in any way they can, through the boosters, concession stand, fund raising or whatever is needed. They care about the team and not just their child. These are parents who get it! They encourage other players whether their child is playing or not. These are dream parents.

THE BAD: This is for those who drop off their child at practice early, then are late picking them up. They may show up for the games or they may not. There is little to no interest in helping the program or team. They are an absentee parent when it comes to sports. I do want to give a disclaimer here there can be many reasons for this, divorce, other children, but the most common one is work. Now days when both parents must work to survive I find this as being the most common. So it is quite unfair to list them here but it's really the only place they fit. If you are one of those parents, I'm sorry; you are missing a big part of your child's life. It's important for the young man or woman to have that support from one of the parents. If you are one of these parents, please take the time to listen to your athlete when they arrive home. Listen to the good and the bad, but above all encourage them and be there for them when you can.

THE UGLY: This is for the parents who are on top of things a little too much. It's for those as one coach described "Over the top." Those who always seem to be in the way. It was funny, two different coaches from two different teams described this parent the same, "Helicopter" parents, who are always hovering around. Now I'm not saying that is a bad thing, to want to watch practices, or drills and even offer your help in the right situations, but the critical issue is do you allow the coach to coach or do you criticize his coaching technique when he's not around. Why do you hover? I will say that I was a hovering parent, but my purpose was to glean all I could from watching practices and listening to the coaches instruct. I knew one day that I would be coaching and I wanted to learn all I could.

These parents are, enablers, with unrealistic expectations and over-critical. This is how the urban dictionary defines enablers: *"ivEnablers tend to fear calling others on their destructive habits because these "others" tend to be friends, family or others close to the enabler."* These parents know it all and are overly critical to coaches, and other players.

Finally one coach had this to say about them, they are idiot parents. Not quite sure I'd go that far, but there has been quite a few that fit this description to a tee.

Being an involved parent shows that you care about the <u>team</u> and not just your child. The team is the most important thing in sports. If it isn't, you must be playing golf.

***

LIFE STORY: There is nothing like volunteering for an organization and once you get involved it's hard to walk away. Why? Because of all the people you get to meet, some good and some not so, but the biggest reasons are the kids. Back a few years ago I was President of the league my child was playing in and the joys of being President was you had to be at the field most of the time, which was no problem for me. Anyway, this one particular evening I was at the field as the players were arriving. I had gotten to know quite a few of them and most would say hi as they ran by. This one young man was always polite and never showed much emotion, just a matter of fact type of attitude. Well this particular evening he came bouncing through the gate with an ear to ear smile. I hollered, "Hey what's with the big smile?" He hollered back, "My Dad is going to be here tonight." He pumped his fist in the air and let out a big "woo hoooo." Now like Paul Harvey, (maybe some don't know who that is) but I will tell you "the rest of the story". His mother was so faithful, showing up at the practices, games and whatever she needed to do for the team or league. His Dad on the other hand was involved with professional sports and had to be away from the family most of the season. So to him it was a big moment for his dad to be able to watch him play. This is the case with most of the children, they love to have their parents there to watch and encourage them.

If you want to have an impact on a lot of kid's lives, get involved in youth sports, give that league a call. Get involved you won't regret it.

CURBING YOUR EMOTION

WOW!!! As I researched this area I couldn't believe how many incidents of parent emotions going overboard there were. While I have had a couple of situations arise with parents, never have I been in a situation like the articles I read. The section before this is "Parents Self-Evaluation" if you didn't read it please go back and read it. If you did read it, maybe re-read it. Some parents are very hard headed and refuse to listen to advice. I hope you're not one of those. It's fun watching your kids play sports and it can get quite emotional and if you can't control it, then simply put, don't attend their games.

Here is a special note to those parents, STOP BEING IDIOTS!! You embarrass yourself and your child. It's simply a game, for KIDS, not parents. When you get out of control you ruin a game that's supposed to be fun.

Here's an example: In her article, [v]*"When Parents Behave Badly at Kids' Sporting Events"*, Katy Abel writes, *"Jeff Leslie still remembers the little girl standing on the mound, trying to play ball."* He explains, *"She was pitching out there and all of a sudden she broke down crying,"* the volunteer president of the Jupiter-Tequesta Athletic Association recalls. *"The coach went out to talk to her and she said, 'My dad is embarrassing me to death.'"* Leslie continues, *"The child, like many others, had a father who spent much of his time during the game yelling and screaming at coaches, and at members of opposing teams."*

How sad, I'm sure none of us want to embarrass our children, but it seems like the times we do that the most is when they are playing sports. So take an honest look at yourself parent, do you have to take a deep breath and control your emotions. Maybe just staying quiet will help, I don't know but you need to figure it out.

So now, how do you curb your emotions? The number one thing is get away from everyone. Don't stay around people, when you feel your emotions beginning take a deep breath and leave, until you can come back and enjoy the game. DO NOT talk to your child during the game, make sure they have all they will need before the game, STAY AWAY, yes this means you too mom.

Cheer for the team and all the players, remember IT'S A GAME!!! When the other team makes a good play let them know. Enjoy the entire game, it makes it more fun. When I began to look at the other players and team differently it took away so much of the energy.

Another thing to try is channel your energy to a positive area--i.e. scout, join Booster Club, help with fundraisers. For those really over the top, have a private meeting to discuss issues.

You must understand that the coaches and refs are going to make mistakes and it's all part of the game. That's what makes it so much fun. Most games are not won or lost by a ref's call, a coach's mistake or an error, bad pass, fumble, missed shot. It's not one play that makes a game. So many times I have heard if we had only made that one play or pitch, or catch. That's what gets us going, look at the game as a whole. Each team, player, coach and ref trying their best to work hard to accomplish the task at hand.

The <u>team</u> is the most important thing.

***

LIFE STORY: While there were plenty of the stories to choose from this was one that touched me and angered me at the same time. This story happened a few years back at an ice hockey practice. It's about two dads who had a disagreement over the practice. It started at a practice, yes a practice, so they were evidently teammates. Clearly parent number one was on the ice supervising the young players, who three of the players were his sons. Parent number two observing the play from off the ice, thought the play was getting a little too rough and yelled at parent one to stop the rough play. A heated conversation ensued and parent number two ran onto the ice. The rink manager interrupted and ordered parent number two to leave, but he came back in. The two men then exchanged blows and parent number two gained the upper hand, beating parent number one unconscious. All this over a youth hockey game, parent number one died two days later. All of this for what? Two families negatively impacted over youth sports, how sad.

Parents the old adage you tell your kids, take it and put it into practice at their games and practices, "You should be seen, and not heard."

ONE FINAL THOUGHT

Again in closing this is not an exhaustive book on parenting an athlete. I hope you were able to glean something from it to help you along the way. But before I close I would be remiss if I didn't say a little more about your child being a Student Athlete. This is where the parent can make all the difference. As your child develops their athletic ability make sure they are developing the academic skills. They do go hand in hand, in fact, academic scholarships help when looking at colleges. As your child grows and starts high school if their love for their sport is still the same and their desire is to play at the next level you can't start looking too soon. It's a big country and a lot of schools to consider. They are little fish in a big pond, don't let them limit themselves. You catch more fish with a net, than with a pole.

The question is how do you do that? Well, my son and I didn't do very well at it. He got the normal bulk letter of interest from over ten colleges, but what do you do with that? I am thankful for the one college that came after him and he signed a letter of intent on Halloween night. If that coach hadn't liked my son so much I don't think he would have played college ball, even being one of the top players in the area. I wish we would have had some help. Look for that help, there are now people out there willing to come alongside and guide and direct right along with promoting your athlete. If you are interested in learning more about this email me at dr68chuck@aol.com.

The benefits of sports outweigh the negatives, so it's the responsibility of parents, schools and others involved in the lives of kids to help make sports a successful and pleasurable experience.

One last quote from my friend the professional athlete; *"I can't imagine what it is like in children's sports now. I have friends that have kids that play and the biggest thing I notice is they need to be grounded. If the kid can play he/she will get noticed. Also in my opinion the greatest thing a kid can do to get a scholarship is take care of things in the classroom. Very few kids will have the opportunity to get into a school on athletics alone, however if they have good grades they will attract the schools who do not have big athletic programs. There are a lot of colleges with athletic programs but they are not big money makers. If a kid has good grades but not as well on the field they are more apt to get an opportunity to play in college because they can get into the schools who are truly looking for student athletes."*

***

LIFE STORY: Time for one final story, this is a combination of two. The first is about a couple with two young boys. The dad

was actively involved in both their sports activities and coached multiple sports teams for each. We became good friends and when I took a team to Cooperstown to play they went with us. He learned the games he coached and was an excellent coach and motivator. While in New York I was hearing some grumbling about playing time and after one of our games he put his hand on my shoulder as we walked and told me to stay the course, that I was doing a great job. This encouraged me to continue down the path and we ended taking 6th out of 64 teams. I tell you this, so I can tell you this, it wasn't long after we got back that he was diagnosed with an advanced form of cancer and passed away. I was asked to perform the memorial services. This man had such an impact on young lives through sports that the young men and ladies came to the service wearing their uniforms. Over a thousand people attended this man's services and most were from the contacts he had made during his life through youth sports. He was a wonderful man and made an impact.

The second story is short. As I have said I have coached numerous teams and levels. So many times I will be out and about and see those young people I coached, some still call me coach others always seem to have a hearty hand shake or hug for me. So in concluding, you can have an impact on the next generation all you have to do is get involved with your local youth sports activities. They are always looking for help and now with the internet it makes it all the easier to find them and contact the person in charge. Don't delay, do it right now, call someone and volunteer to be that coach, team parent, or board member. It's okay to have "the time of your life." Live it up!

---

[i] Cox, R. H. (2002). Sport Psychology: Concepts and Applications (5th ed). Boston: McGraw Hill.

[ii] Fender, L. K. (1989). Athlete burnout: Potential for research and intervention strategies. The Sport Psychologist, 3, 63-71.

[iii] Cresswell, S. L. & Eklund, R. C. (2003). The athlete burnout syndrome: A practitioner's guide. The New Zealand Journal of Sports Medicine, 31, 4-9
Websites used:

http://educatedsportsparent.com/athlete-burnout
[iv] http://www.urbandictionary.com/define.php?term=enabler
[v] http://life.familyeducation.com/sports-parents/behavior/36401.html

www.ingramcontent.com/pod-product-compliance
Lightning Source LLC
Chambersburg PA
CBHW060611030426
42337CB00018B/3044